MIKE THALER'S
RIDDLE RAINBOW

STEER
WARS

IT'S COWSMIC

CARTOON
COW RIDDLES

from The Creator of Letterman

**tempo
books**
GROSSET & DUNLAP
A Filmways Company
Publishers • New York

FOR ROBERT & LOVONNE & AMY

STEERWARS
Cartoon Cow Riddles
Copyright © 1979 by Michael C. Thaler
All Rights Reserved
ISBN: 0-448-17040-X
A Tempo Books Original
Tempo Books is registered
in the U.S. Patent Office
Published simultaneously in Canada
Printed in the United States of America

Cover art and interiors by Michael Horen

What's it called
when cows fight
in outer space?

Steer Wars

Who are
the most famous
cow detectives
on T. V. ?

How do cowboys get on their horses?

With steer-ups

Where do little cows eat?

In calfeterias

Where do
big cows eat?

In resteerants

What do you call
a cow you can sit on?

A cowch

What do you call a dancing cow?

A hoofer

What do you call
a gangster cow?

A mobsteer
or
a moobster

What kind of cows always repeat themselves?

Eccows

What are the two favorite games of little cows?

Moo-nopoly

and Mar-bulls

What is a cow's favorite drink?

Cowfee

What gives milk,
goes moo,
and makes all your
wishes come true?

Your Dairy
Godmother

What cow was a famous astronomer?

Cowpernicus

Where do cows go dancing?

Discowtheques

Where do cows go
for amoosment?

Cowney Island

Where do cows go to get smart?

To cowllege

Where do medieval
noble cows live?

In cowstles

What cow is a famous underwater explorer?

Jacques Cowsteau

What do you call it
when a bunch of
cows won't do
what you tell them?

A mootiny

What do you call
a funny cow?

A cowmedian

What do you call very frightening cows?

Monsteers

Do cows
play records?

No.
They play cowsettes

Knock, knock.
Who's there?
Doubles.
Doubles who?

Doubles is tougher than the cows.

Knock, knock.
Who's there?
Calf.
Calf who?

Take calf a guess.

Knock, knock.
Who's there?
Udder.
Udder who?

Udder people
guessed.

Knock, knock.
Who's there?
Beef.
Beef who?

Beefore I tell you,
let me in.

Knock, knock.
Who's there.
Heifer.
Heifer who?

Heifer you let me in,
I'll tell you.

FAMOUS
COW EVENTS:
Cowsteer's Last Stand
The Losers

The Winners Cowcheese and Sitting Bull*

* shown reclining

Cowlumbus
Discovering America

Humphrey Bullgart
in *Cowsablanca*

Any Bull
crossing the Alps

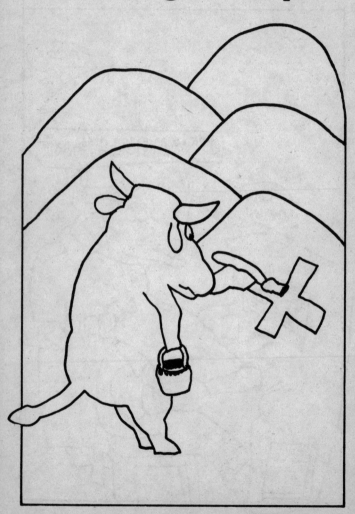

How do cows steer boats?

With rudders

How do cows steer cars?

With steer-in-wheels

What kind of cars do cows drive?

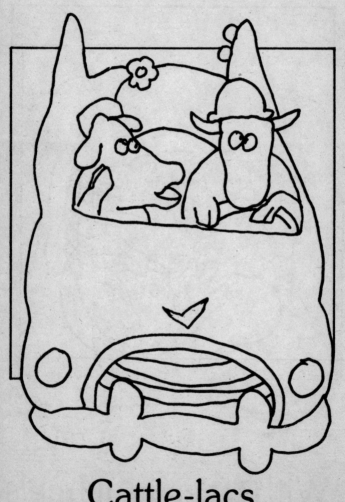

Cattle-lacs

What sport do cows like best?

Basketbull

What do cows ride on?

Moopeds

What kind of cows make pearls?

Oysteers

What cow was a great boxing champion?

Moohammed Ali

What cow was a great singer?

Cowruso

What cow was a great composer?

Moozart

What do you call a Russian cow in outer space?

A cowmunist

What do you call a cow that acts in films?

A movie steer

Where do cows go on vacation?

Cowsta Rica

What country has the most bulls?

Bullgaria

Where do little French cows drink sodas?

In cafes

What do little cows get in their teeth?

Calfities

What disease do little cows get?

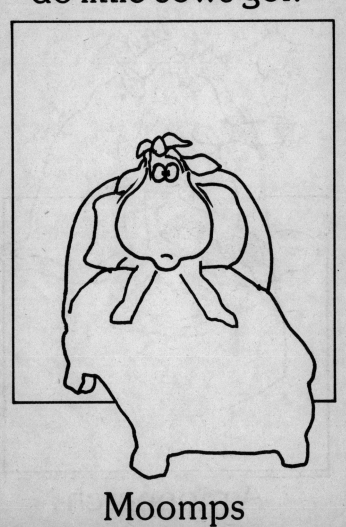

Moomps

What do you call a cow king?

A moonarch

What books do little calves like to read?

Cowmics

Where do you put antique cows?

In mooseums

What do you call ancient Egyptian cows?

Moomies

What do cows wear on their upper lips?

Moostaches

Where do country cows shop?

Steers and Roebuck

What's green and purple and goes moo?

A mootation

What is white and fluffy and goes moo?

Cowds

Who has horns, a red suit and goes moo?

Santa Cows

Knock, knock.
Who's there?
Cattle.
Cattle who?

Cattle meow all night
if you don't let him in.

Knock, knock.
Who's there?
Heifer.
Heifer who?

Heifer you and
heifer me.

Knock, knock.
Who's there?
Heifer.
Heifer who?

Heifer you've gone . . .

An outbreak of hoof-in-mouth
or
a severe case of moombles.

Who are these famous cow artists of moodern art?

1. Moodigliani
2. Moodrian
3. Moonet
4. Kathy Cowitz
5. Picowso
6. Mary Cowsatt
7. Henry Mooer

When are cows the loudest?

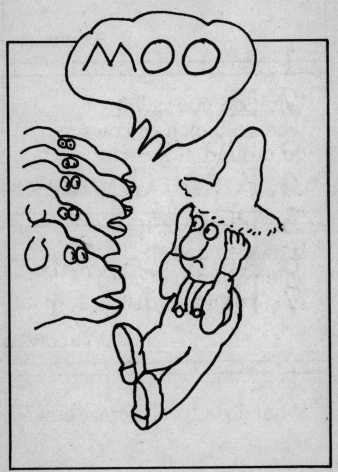

When they're herd

What do you call it when
cows sing together?

A cowrus

What do you call it
when a bunch of cows
go around in a circle?

A cowrousel

What do you call it
when a bunch of cows
swing on a trapeze?

A circows

What do you call a crazy cow?

A mooniac

What do you call it
when cows put on lipstick?

Cowsmetic

When is your leg like a cow?

When it's your calf

What are cow conversations?

Moo-notonous

What little cow was found
in the bullrushes?

Little Mooses

What three states
have the most cows?

Cowlorado, Moosouri
and Cowifornia

How do cows travel?

Cowst to Cowst

What name did they change
Cowstantinople to?

Istanbull

What do you call
a cow's living?

It's breed and butter

Photo by Jone Miller

Mike Thaler is a children's book author, illustrator, cartoonist, sculptor and teacher. He is also a modern day word wizard. His special word magic and cartoon drawings have made children and adults laugh all over the world. In RIDDLE RAINBOW he has taken the riddle to dizzying heights of imagination and fun. He is truly a genius at making children laugh.

All the Books in
MIKE THALER'S
RIDDLE RAINBOW

UNICORNS ON THE COB
What Is It Riddles?
YELLOW 0-448-17043-4

GRIN & BEAR IT
Cartoon Bear Riddles
ORANGE 0-448-17042-6

THE NOSE KNOWS
Cartoon Echo Riddles
RED 0-448-17041-8

STEER WARS
Cartoon Cow Riddles
PURPLE 0-448-17040-X

TOUCANS ON TWO CANS
Cartoon Can Riddles
BLUE 0-448-17039-6

SCREAMERS
Monster Riddles
GREEN 0-448-17038-8